The Fundamentals of
Office 365

Kevin Wilson

www.luminescentmedia.co.uk

The Fundamentals of Office 365

Publisher: Luminescent Media
Director: Kevin Wilson
Lead Editor: Steven Ashmore
Technical Reviewer: Mike Taylor, Robert Ashcroft
Copy Editors: Joanne Taylor, James Marsh
Proof Reader: Linda Holland
Indexer: James Marsh
Cover Designer: Kevin Wilson

eBook versions and licenses are also available for most titles. Any source code or other supplementary materials referenced by the author in this text is available to readers at

www.luminescentmedia.co.uk/resources

For detailed information about how to locate your book's source code, go to

www.luminescentmedia.co.uk/resources

Acknowledgements

Thanks to all the staff at Luminescent Media for their passion, dedication and hard work in the preparation and production of this book.

To all my friends and family for their continued support and encouragement in all my writing projects.

To all my colleagues, students and testers who took the time to test procedures and offer feedback on the book

Finally thanks to you the reader for choosing this book. I hope it helps you to use your computer with greater ease.

About the Author

Kevin Wilson, a practicing computer engineer and tutor, has had a passion for gadgets, cameras, computers and technology for many years.

After graduating with masters in computer science, software engineering & multimedia systems, he has worked in the computer industry supporting and working with many different types of computer systems, worked in education running specialist lessons on film making and visual effects for young people. He has also worked as an IT Tutor, has taught in colleges in South Africa and as a tutor for adult education in England.

His books were written in the hope that it will help people to use their computer with greater understanding, productivity and efficiency. To help students and people in countries like South Africa who have never used a computer before. It is his hope that they will get the same benefits from computer technology as we do.

Table of Contents

Microsoft Outlook 2013 104

Chapter 1

Cloud Computing

The "cloud" was originally a metaphor for the internet and many network diagrams represented the internet with a symbol of a cloud. As internet services became more advanced, the cloud became a set of hardware devices such as data servers, application servers all connected to networks with large storage space providing services such as applications including microsoft word, email and disk storage for documents. These cloud services include the delivery of software and storage space over the Internet based on user demand having as little as possible stored on the user's machines.

If you have an account with a Web-based e-mail service like Hotmail or Gmail, then you've had some experience with the cloud. Instead of running an e-mail program on your computer, you log in to a Web e-mail account remotely. The software and storage for your account doesn't exist on your computer it's on the cloud. The idea is to be able to access your applications, services and files from anywhere, whether at the office or out and about.

This has become a huge advantage as data can be stored centrally making back ups easier. Applications and servers can be built and maintained centrally by dedicated support staff making downtime a minimum. Plus all your data and services can be accessed from anywhere thanks to wireless devices such as tablets, smartphones, laptops and PCs.

Office 365 is Microsoft's cloud based service and is a subscription-based version of Office 2013. Unlike any of the traditional Office suites such as Office 2010, Office 365 allows you to install Office applications on up to five different computers. It includes some additional features, such as Office on Demand, 20 GB of additional online storage space through SkyDrive, and the option to install Office 2011 on Mac computers.

Chapter 1: Cloud Computing

Office 365 subscription guarantees that you'll be able to upgrade to the latest version of Office whenever it's available at no additional cost, which can save you a lot of money over time.

Because Office 365 is paid by either an annual or monthly subscription fee, you'll need to be able to manage your account settings, including payment information.

Setting up Office 365

Office 365 is a subscription-based version of Office 2013. Unlike any of the traditional Office suites such as Office 2010, Office 365 allows you to install Office applications on up to five different computers. It includes some additional features, such as Office on Demand, 20 GB of additional online storage space through SkyDrive, and the option to install Office 2011 on Mac computers.

Office 365 subscription guarantees that you'll be able to upgrade to the latest version of Office whenever it's available at no additional cost, which can save you a lot of money over time.

Because Office 365 is paid by either an annual or monthly subscription fee, you'll need to be able to manage your account settings, including payment information.

There are a number of different options and packages available depending on what your needs are.

Office Home & Student - can be installed on one PC and includes, word, excel, powerpoint and onenote.

Office University - A 4-year subscription at a great value of £1.25 a month and can be installed on 2 PCs or Macs. Has word, excel, powerpoint, outlook, one note, access and publisher.

Office Professional - can be installed on one PC and is aimed more at business users, the package includes, word, excel, powerpoint, one note, outlook, publisher and access.

Office 365 Home Premium - can be installed on 5 PCs or Macs plus upto 5 mobile devices. This package is aimed at home users with more than one computer. The package includes word, excel, powerpoint, outlook, one note, access and publisher.

Here is a comparison summary according to Microsoft's website.

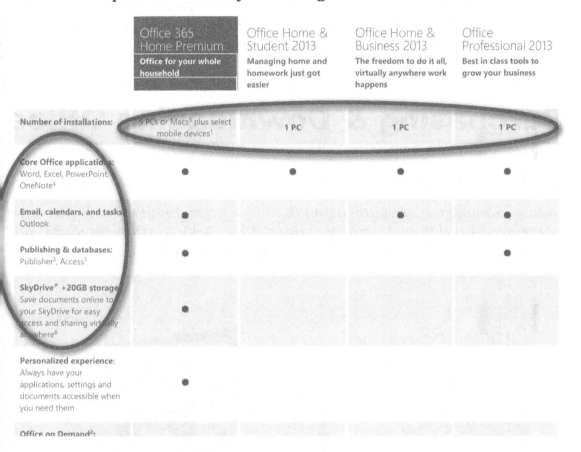

Which Version is Right for Me?

If you're still not sure which version of Office you want, take some time to think about the features that are most important to you and how they fit into your budget. Below are some questions you may want to ask yourself:

* Do I just need Word, Excel, and PowerPoint, or do I need the entire Office suite? If you only need the core Office applications, it may be best to buy Office Home & Student, since it's the cheapest option over the long term.

- If you need advanced programs like Access, you'll need either Office Professional or Office 365 Home Premium.

- Do I want to install Office on more than one computer? If your household has several computers, you may want to get an Office 365 Home Premium subscription. The non-subscription editions can only be installed on one computer, so you would need to buy multiple copies.

- Will I do a lot of editing on the go? If you use a lot of public computers at libraries or business centres, Office 365 Home Premium may be your best option, since it includes Office on Demand. However, keep in mind that you can do basic editing with the free Office Web Apps, even if you don't own a copy of Office.

Purchasing & Downloading Office

First go to microsoft office website

office.microsoft.com/store

In this example we are purchasing the home premium version. If you want to download a different version change it by clicking 'office products' and selecting the version from the drop down box. The procedure is the same.

Click buy now.

You can either pay a monthly subscription or pay an annual cost. Choose depending on your budget. Paying monthly will spread the cost over the year rather than paying one lump sum.

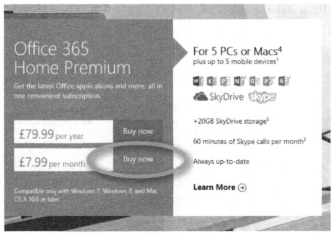

Select 'buy now'. In this example I am going to pay monthly. Click 'review and checkout'

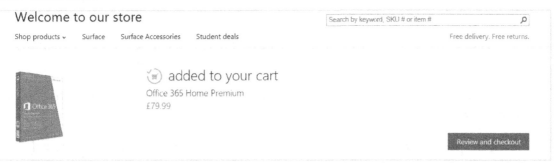

Click 'next'. Sometimes depending on your country you might also see 'checkout'. Click to confirm your order.

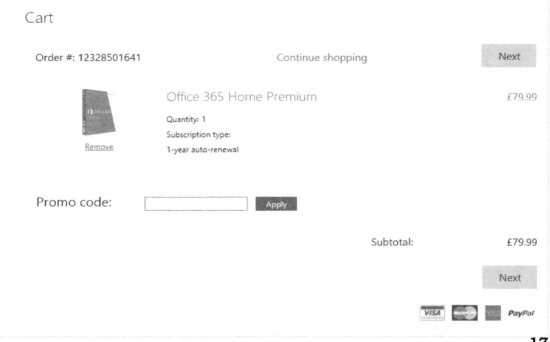

Chapter 2: Setting up Office 365

Once you have done that you will be prompted to sign in with your microsoft account.

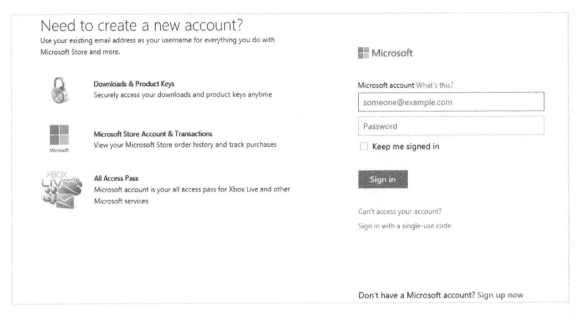

If you haven't got a microsoft account, click 'sign up now' and follow the instructions.

You will be prompted to enter your payment details. If you have purchased from the microsoft store before then you can choose to pay with an existing card or you can add a different card number.

Enter your information in all the fields then click next at the bottom of the screen then review and confirm your order.

Microsoft Accounts

If you are using Windows 8 you will probably already have a Microsoft account that you created when you set up your machine. This is usually the username/email and password you used to sign into windows 8. Or you may already have one, if you do you can skip this section.

If this is not the case then you can quickly create one. To set up a Microsoft Account you need to go to the website below and sign up

`signup.live.com`

You will see a form asking for your details.

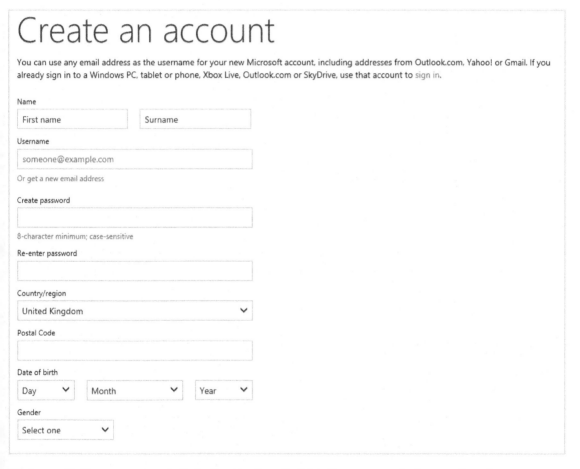

Enter all the required details in the fields then scroll down the form.

Once you have filled in all the details click 'create account' at the bottom

Installing Office 365

Once you have purchased the software you will need to sign in with your microsoft account.

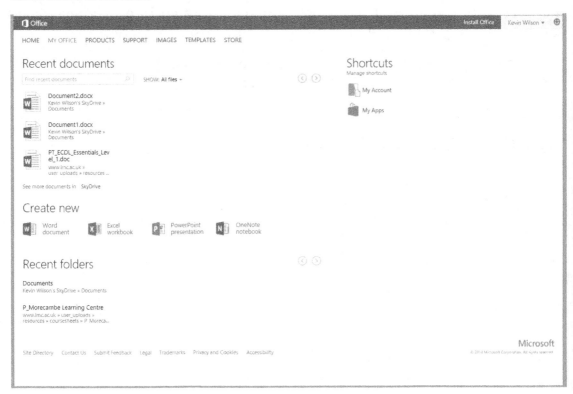

To install office 365 on your computer, click 'my account'. Select 'office for windows' from the drop-down box circled below then click install.

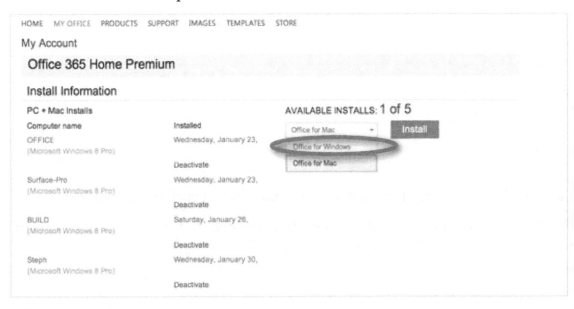

If you are prompted click run install the download. Microsoft Office 365 will download and install the office applications onto your computer. This can take a while to complete depending on the speed of your computer and your internet connection.

Once the download and install is complete and if this is not your computer and belongs to someone else in the family, open up an office application such as microsoft word and select a blank document.

If this is your own computer then you can skip this step.

Click file from the top left hand side and from the screen that appears, shown below, select 'account'.

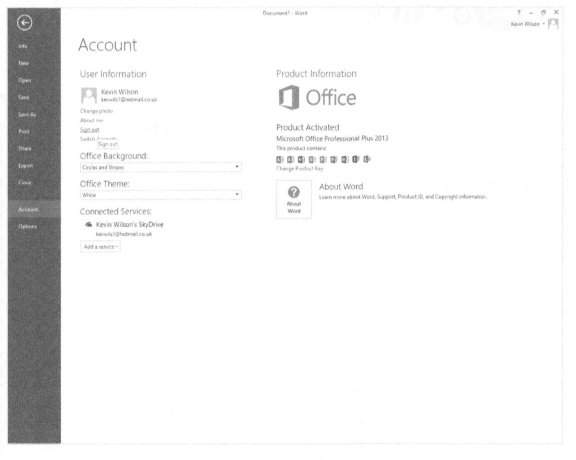

In the main window, Click on 'sign out'

This will allow that person to sign in using their own microsoft account, rather than using yours.

Exchange Email on your iPhone

Tap Settings > Mail, Contacts, Calendars > Add Account.

Tap Microsoft Exchange.

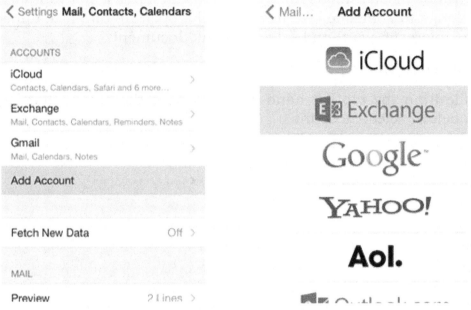

Domain box can be left blank.

Enter your microsoft account email and password

Tap Next on the upper-right corner of the screen. The mail app will automatically detect settings for server names etc.

If your iPhone doesn't automatically detect the settings you can enter them manually

> Server name for IMAP and POP is **outlook.office365.com**

> Server name for SMTP is **smtp.office365.com**.

> Exchange ActiveSync server name is **outlook.office365.com**

These settings can be used if you are using the latest version of Office 365.

Select what information you want to synchronize or copy between your phone and office 356. Eg by default, Mail, Contacts, and Calendar information are synchronized.

If you're prompted to create a passcode, tap Continue and type a numeric passcode.

If you don't set up a passcode, you can't view your email account on your iPhone. You can set up a passcode later your iPhone settings.

Set up Email on Windows Phone

On Start, swipe left to the App list, select Settings, and then select email accounts.

Select add an account

Select Outlook.

Enter your email address and password, then select Sign in. Windows Phone will set up your email account automatically.

If your phone doesn't automatically detect the settings you can enter them manually

Exchange ActiveSync server name is **outlook.office365.com**

These settings can be used if you are using the latest version of Office 365.

Select what information you want to synchronize or copy between your phone and Office 356. Eg by default, Mail, Contacts, and Calendar information are synchronized.

Setting up Outlook Desktop App

When you first start the Outlook application you will be asked to enter your email address, password and sometimes your mail settings.

Click Next, then click Yes to the question "Do you want to set up Outlook to connect to an email account?"

 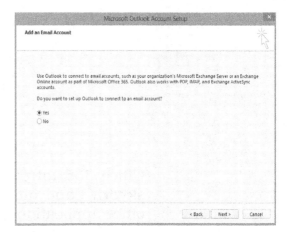

Then click Next to get to the following screen (Add Account). In "Auto Account Setup" enter your name, email address and Password for your office 365 account.

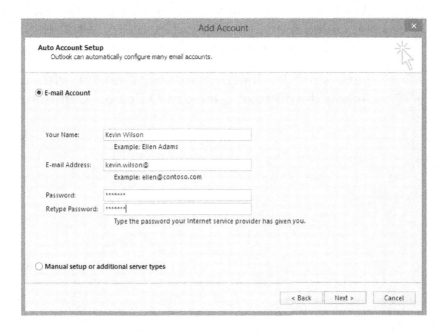

Click Next. Microsoft Outlook will scan the email address you have entered and enter all the server and mail settings for you.

Chapter 3

Using Office 365

Office 365 introduces a number of new apps such as skydrive and also the way you can access your usual office applications such as word, excel or powerpoint.

In this section we will take a look at using Office on Demand and how to get started with it, plus a look at Office Web Apps and what they are.

Also we will be looking at SkyDrive or OneDrive as it will be called shortly and SkyDrive Pro. What the differences are and how to get up and running using them correctly.

Lets start by logging onto our portal with a Microsoft Account and take a look at Office on Demmand.

Office on Demand

A great feature included with Office 365 is Office on Demand, which allows you to stream full-featured versions of most Office applications temporarily to another computer.

This can be especially convenient if you need to edit Office files on a computer that does not have Office installed, such as a public computer in a library or business centre.

All these can be accessed from your account page on under Office on Demand as shown below.

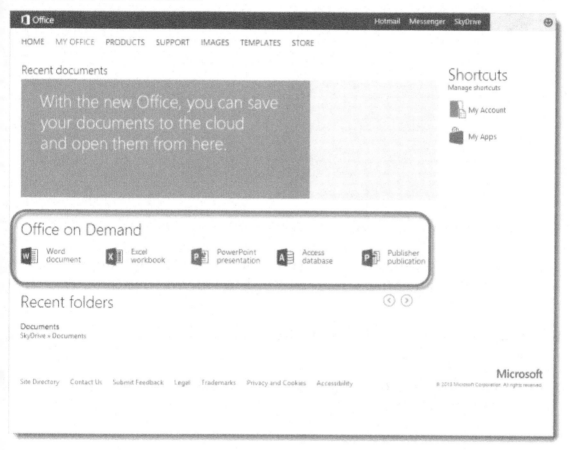

Log onto

www.office.com

Enter your microsoft account email and password, then click 'my office' along the top of the screen.

If you want to use word, click the 'word document' or if you want to start a powerpoint, click the icons under the 'office on demand' section circled above.

Chapter 3: Using Office 365

When you do this you may get a prompt similar to the one below, depending on how the computer is set up and which web browser you're using.

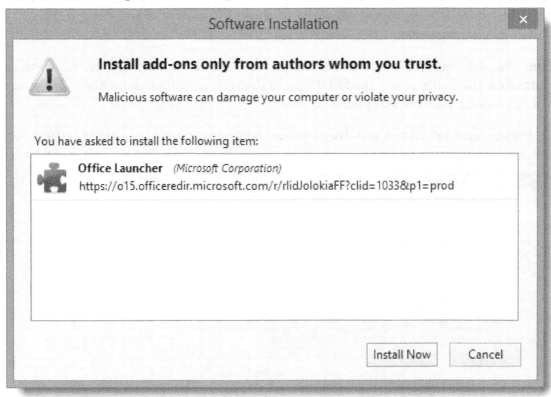

This is just telling you that office 365 needs to install an add on to allow your microsoft applications such as word to run on that computer. Just click 'install now'

When prompted, log in with your Microsoft account email and password and begin using Office.

You can use these versions as you would your standard office applications, they are fully functional.

Office Web Apps

Office web apps allow you to run basic cut down versions of office apps such as Word within your web browser as shown below.

All your edited documents are stored on your skydrive and can be accessed from your account page on

www.office.com

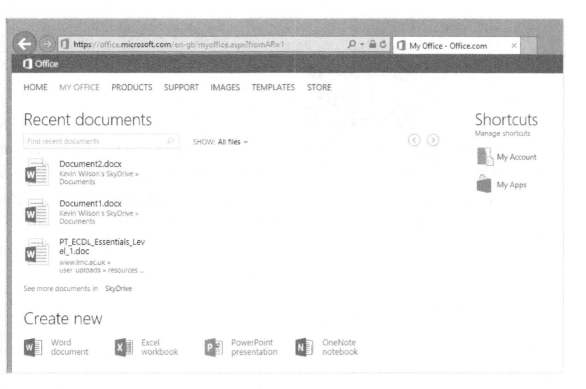

You can open the web apps in a similar fashion as for 'office on demand', except choose an application under the 'create new' section.

As you can see these versions only have the basic editing features of the full scale office applications.

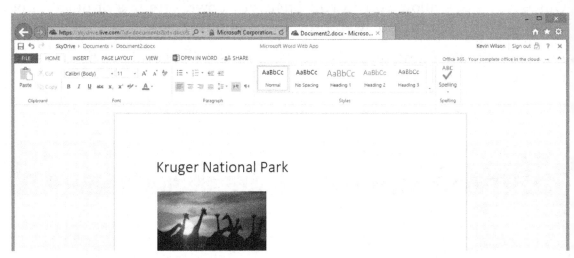

If you have Word 2013 installed on your computer you can click 'open in word' to edit the document with the fully featured application.

Web apps are great if you want to make a few quick adjustments on the fly or perhaps run a powerpoint on a machine that doesn't have powerpoint installed.

SkyDrive/OneDrive

SkyDrive is an online storage area you can use as your own personal online hard drive dubbed cloud storage. It has two versions. One is just called skydrive and is aimed at consumers or home uses. The other version is SkyDrive Pro which is aimed at business and power users.

SkyDrive however, will soon be renamed to OneDrive, after a court ruled that the SkyDrive name infringed on the trademark 'Sky' owned by British Broadcasting Group BSkyB.

SkyDrive is becoming a key product in Microsoft's long-term strategy, as the company continues its transition to mobile devices and cloud based services. SkyDrive is also part of new product releases such as Office 365 and Microsoft Accounts. It is integrated into Windows 8.1 to allow users to save files in the cloud with just a few taps or clicks.

When you create a document with one of the Web Apps, it is saved to your SkyDrive. You can store other files there, too such as photos. Since Web Apps and SkyDrive are based in the cloud, you can access them from any device with an internet connection, at any time.

You can access your skydrive online by logging in with your Microsoft account at

`www.skydrive.com`   **or**   `www.onedrive.com`

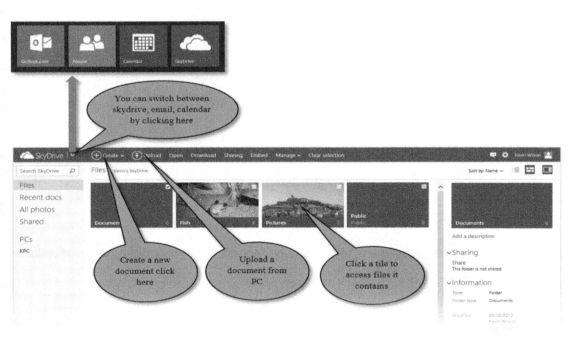

Create a Document

You can create a new document by clicking on create.

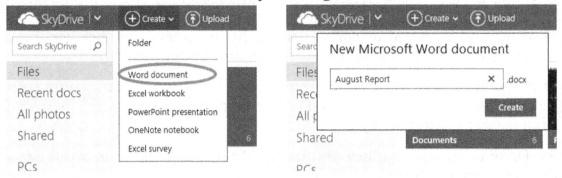

In the 'new microsoft word document' box type in a meaningful name for your document.

Once you have done that. A bank document will open in Word WebApp where you can edit your document and then save to your skydrive.

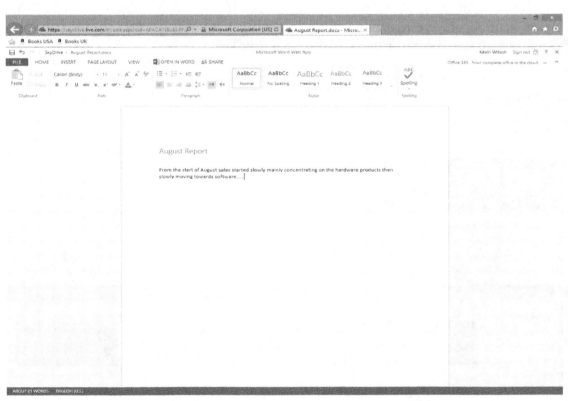

Share a Document

To share documents with someone click the top right of the tile representing the document you want to share. This adds a tick to the box which means it has been selected. Once you have done that click sharing from the top menu.

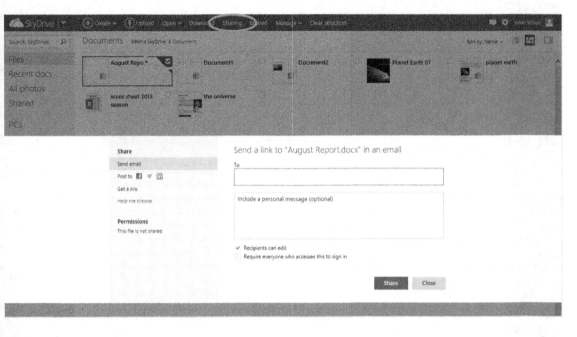

Fill in the details of the recipient's Microsoft account email address. The recipient can log into their Microsoft account and begin editing the document.

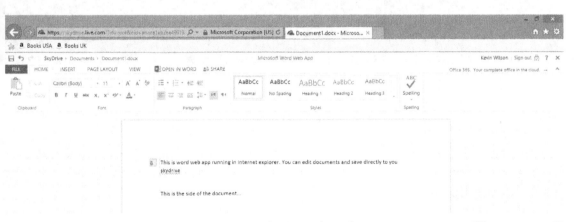

When more than one person is editing the document you will see small icons next to paragraphs indicating that someone is editing that part of the document as shown above.

SkyDrive on your Desktop

You can also access your skydrive from your desktop on your PC or laptop. In Windows 8.1 this has been integrated into windows itself.

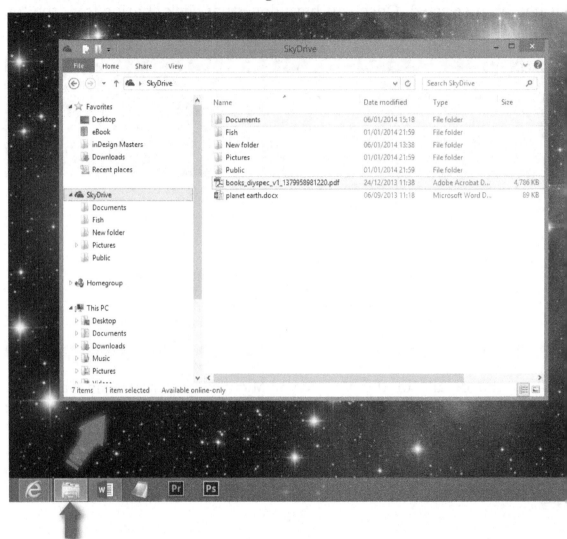

You can upload files from your PC using the windows file explorer

Locate the file on your computer that you wish to upload to your SkyDrive using Windows File Explorer, in this case the file I want is located in the Documents library.

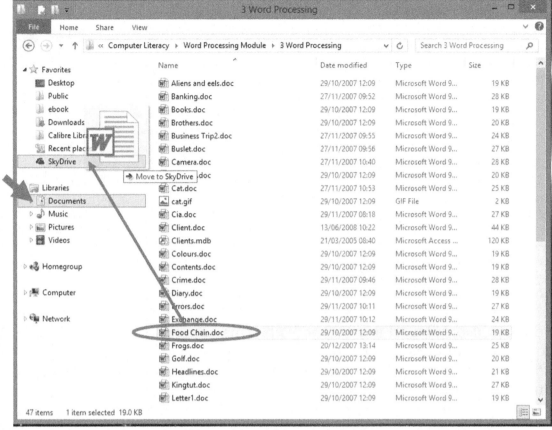

Then click and drag the file to the SkyDrive folder as shown in the image above.

If you know the names of the documents you can use the search feature to locate them quickly. Select the location to search in. In this example I want to search for files in the documents library. So select documents under the 'this pc' or 'libraries' section in the left hand pane as shown below. Then type the name of the document in the 'search documents' field. This will bring up a list of all documents containing the word you typed.

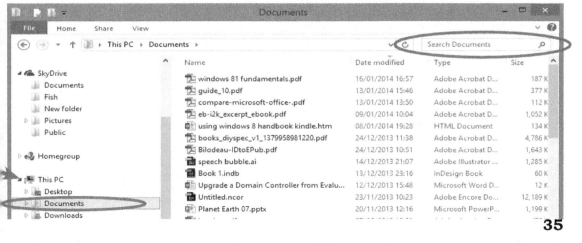

To add them to your skydrive just drag and drop the file as show below.

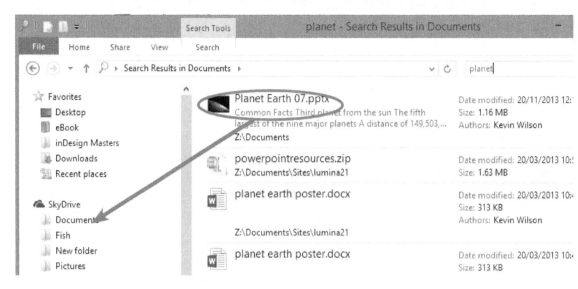

You can also upload Files on the Web. This can be useful if you are on a computer that doesn't have the SkyDrive app or the same version of office as you have. You can upload the file by signing into your SkyDrive account at

www.skydrive.com

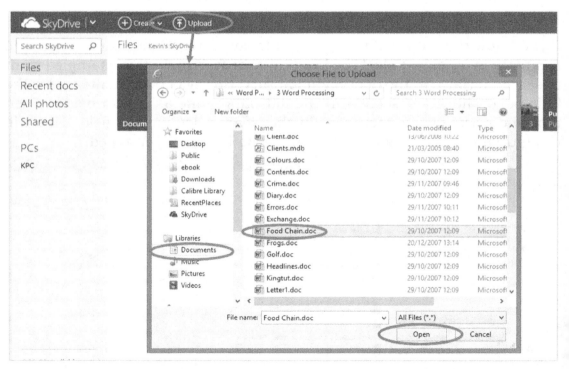

On your home screen click upload and in the dialog box that appears select the files you want to upload.

In this case I want my 'food chain.doc' file uploaded.

To select multiple files hold down the ctrl key while you select your files.

SkyDrive Pro

If a company you work for provided you with an email address or office 365 account, or perhaps you attend college or university, you would be using SkyDrive Pro. SkyDrive Pro will soon be renamed 'OneDrive for Business'

At the time of writing you get 25Gb of storage space for you to add files

You can access your account by going to

```
portal.microsoftonline.com
```

Enter your email address and password for your office 365 account given to you by your company or college etc.

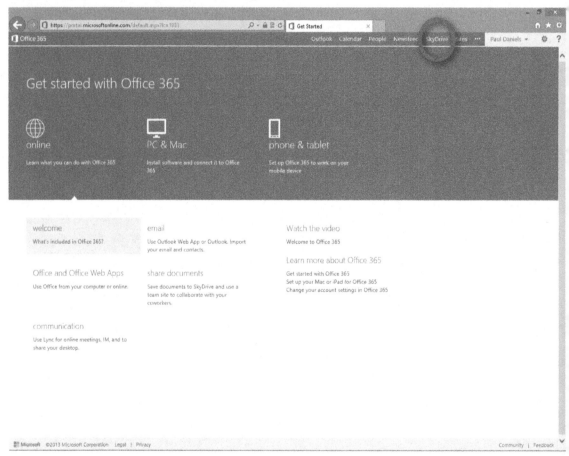

From here you can check your email, view or edit your files and share documents.

To start using SkyDrive Pro click on the SkyDrive icon on the top right of the menu bar circled above.

If this is the first time you have clicked this, Office 365 will take a few moments to set up your account.

Once it has finished you will see your main screen as shown below. From here you can create new documents, share documents and edit them.

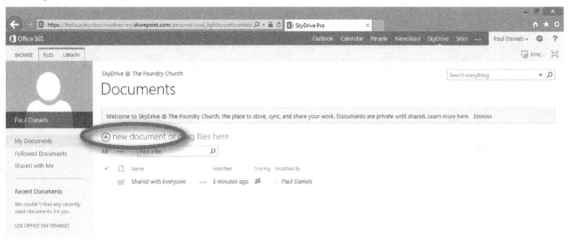

Ribbon Menus

There are ribbon menus hidden in SkyDrive Pro but you can easily access them by clicking on the tabs on the top left of your screen.

The files ribbon allows you to create new files, upload files and share them with colleagues

The library ribbon is less frequently used but allows to add tags, change settings and layout of your SkyDrive.

Create a Document

To create documents using the web portal of skydrive pro click on "new document" and select the type of file you want to create. This could be an excel spreadsheet or a PowerPoint presentation. In this example I am going to use a word document.

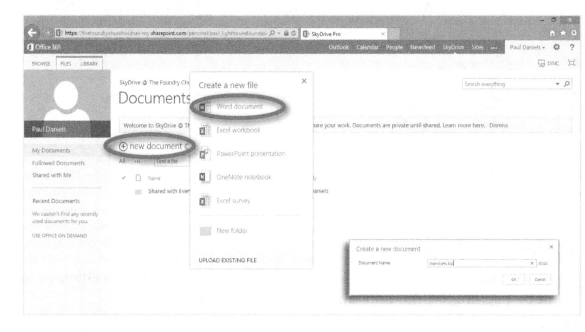

Give your document a meaningful name. Since mine is a list of members I am going to call it "members list".

From here you can edit your document on the web as if it were on Microsoft Word on your machine.

If you have Microsoft Word 2013 installed on your machine you can click "open in word" to edit the document.

Share a Document

To share a document with a colleague, select the document(s) you want by clicking the tick next to the document's icon, as shown below.

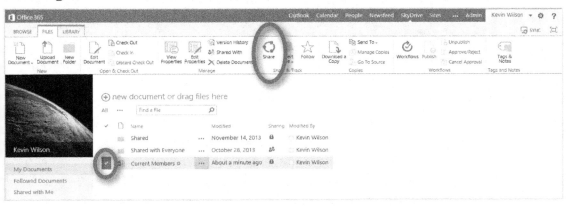

Then click the 'files' tab on the top left hand side of the screen.

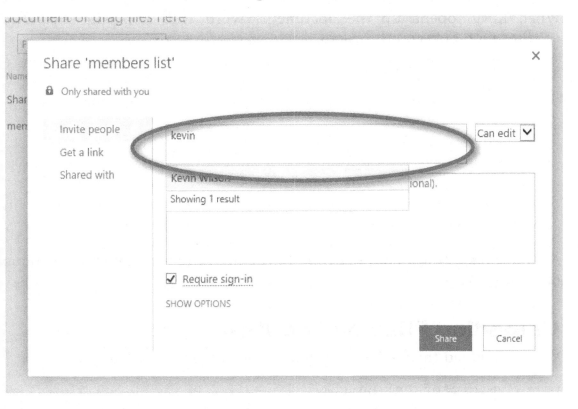

In the box that appears enter the email addresses of the people you want to share the document with.

Also allow the people to edit the document or restrict to read only. You can set this by clicking in the 'can edit' drop down box.

Below is the email sent to Kevin. This is the email the people you have shared your document with would get

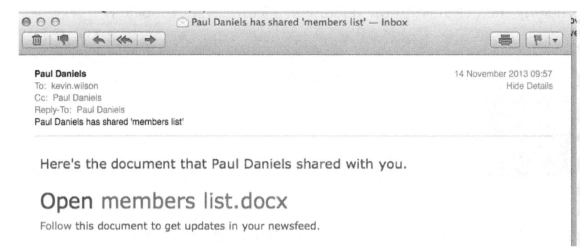

When Kevin opens up the document, Word Web App will show the collaboration between the users.

As you can see below both Paul and Kevin are working on different sections of the document.

Uploading Files on the Web

You can upload the file by signing into your SkyDrive account at

`portal.microsoftonline.com`

On your home screen select skydrive from the menu along the top of the screen. Click Files and in the menu ribbon that appears select upload.

To select multiple files hold down the Ctrl key while you select your files.

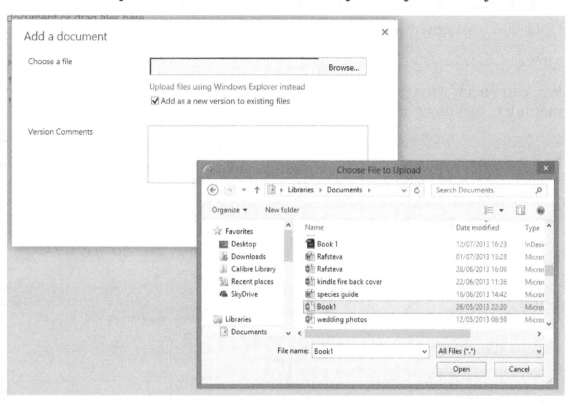

Once uploaded it will appear in your home screen.

You can now edit this document online anywhere using office on demand, office web apps or even microsoft office application installed on another PC or device.

Check your Email Online

Once you are signed into your account using

`portal.microsoftonline.com`

You can check your email by clicking on the outlook icon on the top of the menu bar as shown below

This will take you to Outlook's main screen.

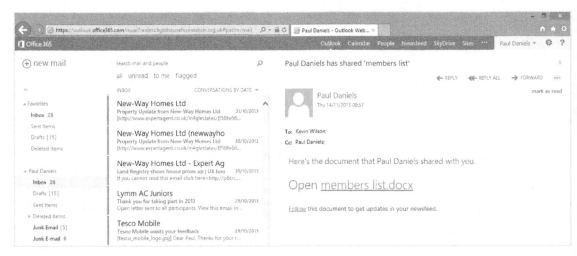

From here you can write a new email by clicking "New Mail", you can read any of your emails in the inbox list by clicking on them - the email you click on will be shown in the email reading pane on the right hand side of the window.

From here click reply to compose a reply to the email.

Chapter 4

Microsoft Word 2013

Microsoft Word is a word processing application that allows you to create many different types of document, from letters, Resumes/CVs to greetings cards, posters and flyers all from a library of customisable templates or from scratch.

Word 2013 gives you the ability to do more with your word processing projects, with the introduction of several enhanced features, such as the ability to create and collaborate on documents online using SkyDrive.

Your first step in creating a document in Word 2013 is to choose whether to start from a blank document or to let a template do much of the work for you.

From then on, the basic steps in creating and sharing documents are the same.

Powerful editing and reviewing tools help you work with others to make your document perfect

Lets begin by launching Word 2013

Starting Word

To launch Word go to the start screen and select "Word 2013".

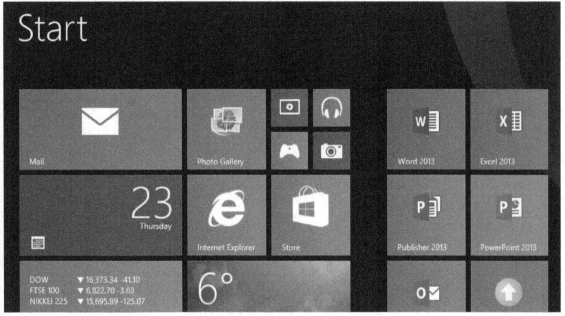

Once Word has loaded, you can select a document from a wide variety of templates, eg brochures, CVs, letters, flyers, etc. If you want to create your own just select blank. Your recently saved documents are shown on the blue pane on the left hand side.

You can also search for a particular template using the search field.

Getting Around Word

Once you select a template, you will see your main work screen.

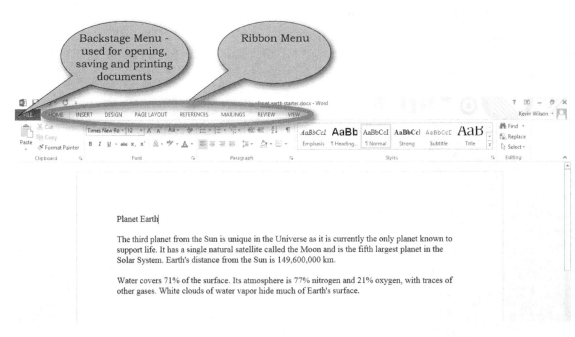

All the tools used in Microsoft word are organised into ribbons loosely based on their function, circled above.

Lets take a closer look.

The Home Ribbon

You will find your text formatting tools here for making text bold, changing style, font, paragraph alignment etc.

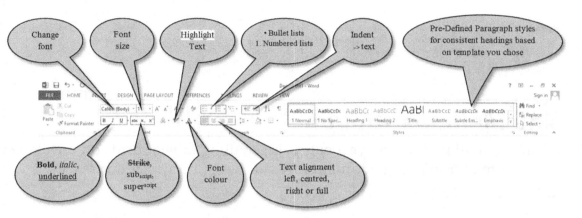

The Insert Ribbon

This is where you will find your clipart, tables, pictures, page breaks, and pretty much anything you would want to insert into a document.

The Design Ribbon

Anything to do with pre-set themes and formatting such as headings, colours and fonts that you can apply to your document and word will automatically format your document according to the themes.

The Page Layout Ribbon

This ribbon you will find your page sizes, margins, page orientation (landscape or portrait) and anything to do with how your page is laid out.

The References Ribbon

This is where you can add automatically generated tables of contents, indexes, footnotes to your documents

The Mailings Ribbon

From the mailings ribbon you can print mailing labels, print on envelopes and create mail-merge documents from a list of names & addresses.

Basic Text Formatting

To format the document we are going to use the formatting tools. These are on the home ribbon shown below.

Using Paragraph Styles

Word has a number of paragraph styles that are useful to keep your formatting consistent. For example you can set a font style, size and colour for a heading or title style...

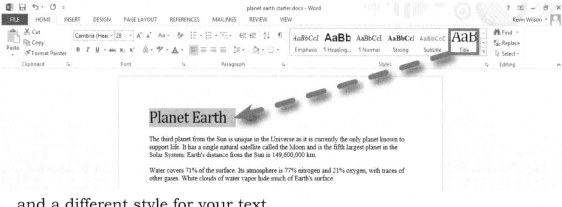

...and a different style for your text.

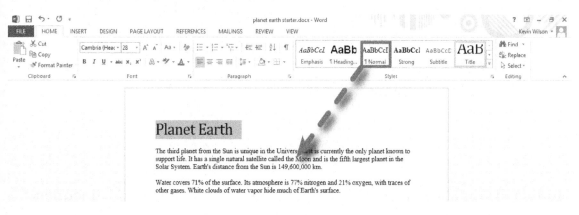

This makes it easier to format your document so you don't have to apply the same font style, size and colour manually every time you want to a heading.

All the styles are pre-set

To set the styles for a heading or paragraph, just highlight it with your mouse as shown below.

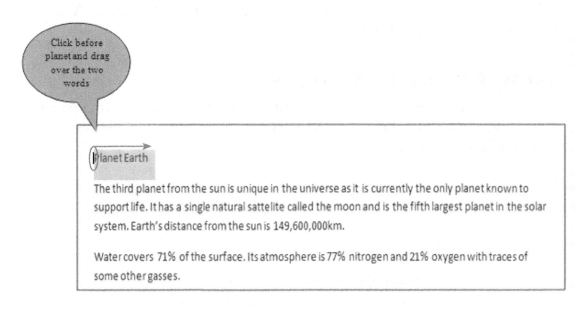

Once you have the text highlighted select a style from the home ribbon.

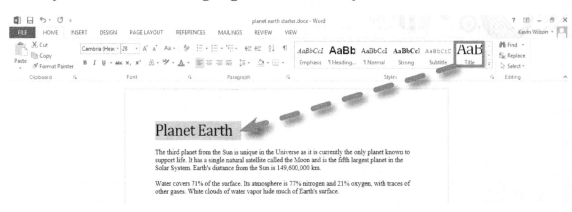

In this example I will use the title style for the heading of my document.

Cut, Copy & Paste

To ease editing documents, you can use copy, cut and paste to move paragraphs or pictures around in different parts of your document.

First select the paragraph below with your mouse by clicking before the word 'white' and dragging your mouse across the paragraph towards the word 'surface' in the same paragraph, as shown opposite.

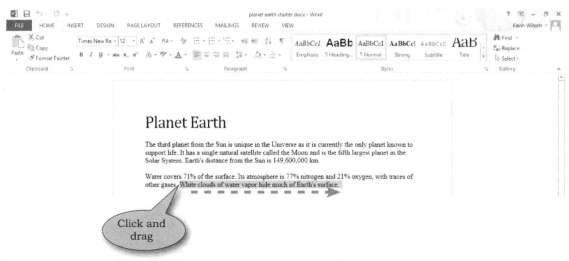

Once you have done that, click 'cut' from the left hand side of your home ribbon. This will 'cut out' the paragraph.

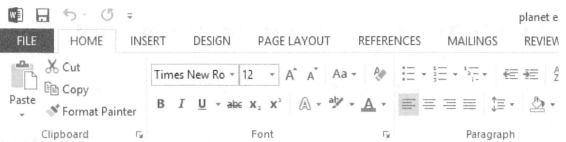

Now click on the location you want the paragraph you just cut out to go

Once you have done that click 'paste' from the home ribbon.

If you wanted to copy something ie make a duplicate of the text, then use the same procedure except click 'copy' instead of 'cut'.

Bold, Italic, Underlined

You can use **bold**, *italic* or <u>underlined</u> text to emphasise certain words or paragraphs. Select the text you want to apply formatting to. For example, to make the text "77% nitrogen" and "21 % oxygen" bold, select them with the mouse and click the bold icon on your home ribbon.

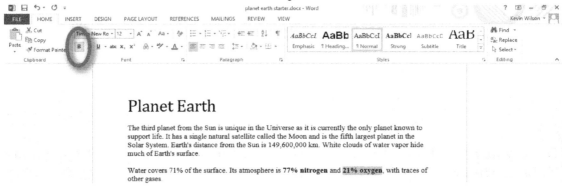

Justify Text: Left, Centred, Right, Full

You can align text to different margins.

Most text will be **left aligned** as demonstrated in this paragraph. Only the left margin is aligned, the right margin is not.

Text can also be **right aligned**
this is good for addresses on the top of letters

Text can also be **fully justified**. This means that the left and right margins are both aligned. This helps when creating documents with images as the text will line up neatly around the image.

Select the text you want to apply formatting to. In this example, I want to make the paragraphs fully justified. This means the text is aligned both the left and right margins.

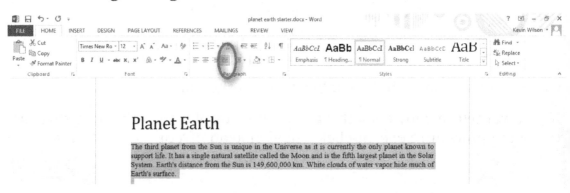

Select the text and in the home ribbon select the fully justify icon.

Adding Images

To add images to your document is easy.

There are two types.

- Your own photos and pictures.

- Clipart. This is a large library of images that can be used in your documents.

The easiest way to add your own photographs or pictures is to find them in your explorer window and drag them on top of your document.

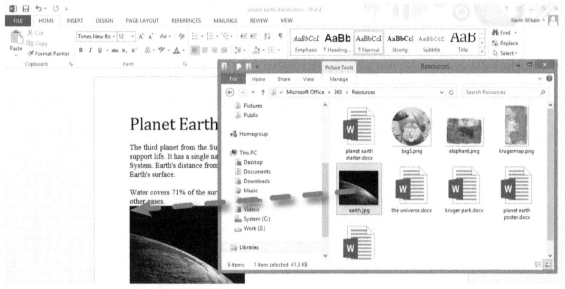

You may need to resize the image, as sometimes they can come in a bit big.

To do this click on the image, you'll see small handles appear on each corner of the image.

These are called resize handles and you can use them by clicking and dragging a corner toward the centre of the image to make it smaller as shown below.

Adding Clipart

Carrying on with our document, I want to add a new section called "World Population" and I want some clipart to illustrate this.

First click the position in your document where you want the clipart to appear.

World Population

The human population of the world is estimated by the United States Census Bureau to be 6,821,600,000. The world population has been growing continuously since the end of the Black Death around 1400.

To insert clipart go to your insert ribbon and click 'online pictures'.

Then in the dialog box type in what you are looking for, as shown below.

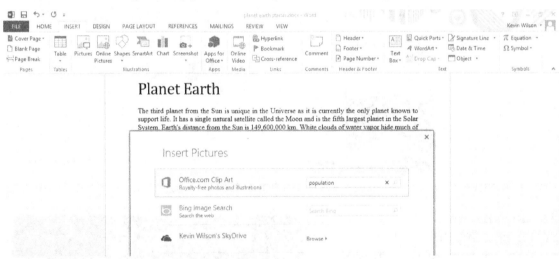

In the search results, click the image you want then click insert

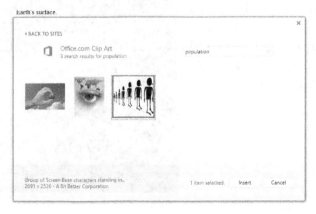

Formatting Images

When you click on your image another ribbon appears called Format. This allows you to add effects and layout your pictures on your page.

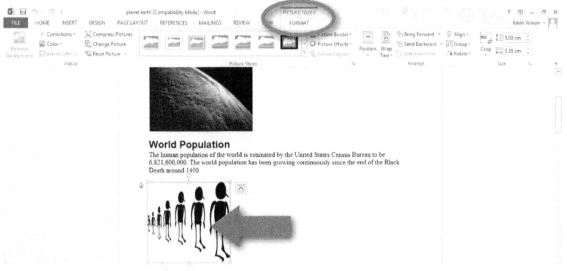

The first thing we want to do is change the text wrapping. Text wrapping enables you to surround a picture or diagram with text.

To do this, click on your image and click the format ribbon.

Click Wrap Text. Then select square. This wraps the text squarely around the image.

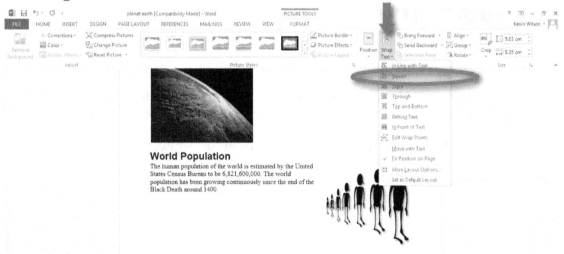

You can now move the image into the correct position, when you do this you will find the text will wrap itself around the image.

Do this with the photograph as well.

Adding Effects to Images

To add effects to your images, such as shadows and borders, click on your image then select the Format ribbon.

In this example, click on the population image.

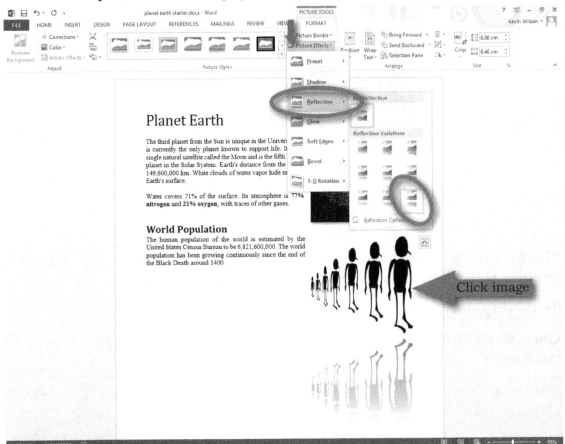

I want to create a nice reflection style to the image. To do this click 'picture effects', then 'reflection' then select a variation as shown above.

Try different effects, such as 'shadow', 'bevel' or 'glow'.

See what affect they have...

Cropping Images

If you insert an image into your document and it has unwanted parts or you want to concentrate on one particular piece of the picture you can crop your image

First drag and drop an image from your pictures library into your document as shown below

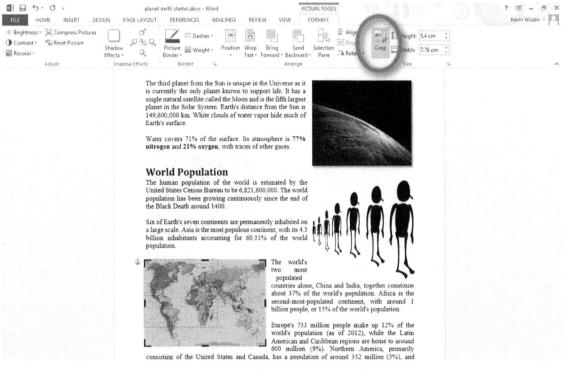

To crop the image, click on the image and click the format ribbon, from the format ribbon click the crop icon circled above.

If you look closely at your image you will see crop handles around the edges of the image.

Click and drag these around the part of the image you want. Eg, I just want to show Africa in the image.

The dark grey bits will be removed to leave the bit of the image inside the crop square

Adding Tables

We have added some more text about world population to our document. Now we want to add a table to illustrate our text.

To insert a table click on your document where you want the table to appear. In this example I want it to appear just below world population paragraph.

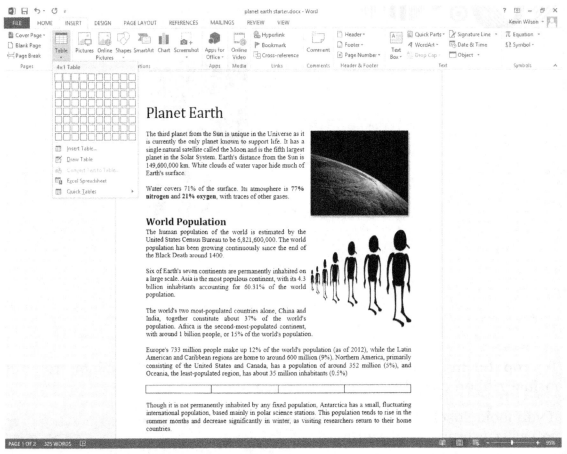

Go to your insert ribbon and select table.

In the grid that appears highlight the number of rows and columns you want. For this table, 1 row and 4columns.

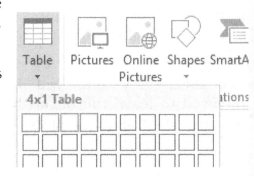

This will add a table with 1 rows & columns to your document.

Now just fill in the table. To move between cells on the table press the tab key. When you get to the end of the row, pressing tab will insert a new row.

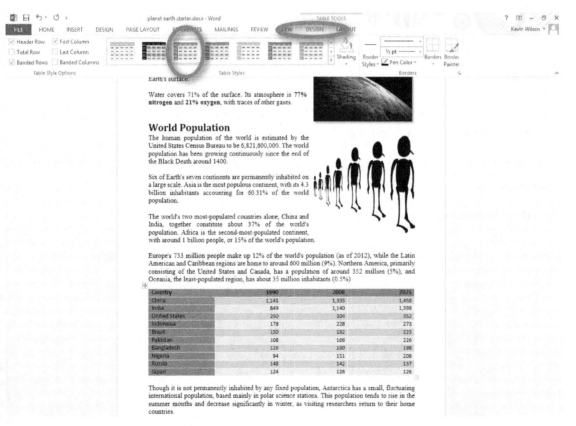

When working with tables, two new ribbons appear, design and layout.

The design tab allows you to select pre-set designs for your table such as column and row shading, borders etc.

For this table I am going to choose one with blue headings and shaded rows.

Click any cell in the table and click the design ribbon. From the designs select one you like.

Save your Work

To save your work, click the small disk icon in the top left hand corner of the screen

In the save as screen, you need to tell word where you want to save the document.

Save it onto "Computer" and in "My Documents" folder, as shown above. Click 'browse' if it isn't there

You can also save onto your SkyDrive by clicking 'SkyDrive' instead of 'Computer'.

Word will ask you what you want to call the file.

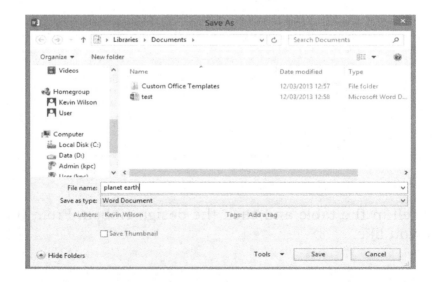

Think of a meaningful name describing the work. In this case "Planet Earth"

Click Save.

Chapter 5

Microsoft Power Point 2013

Microsoft PowerPoint allows you to create multimedia presentations that include animation, narration, images, and videos all from a library of pre designed templates or from a blank canvas.

PowerPoint can be used to create presentations for your up coming sales pitch. Perhaps you are giving a lecture on a specific subject or feeding back information in a meeting. All these can be enhanced using PowerPoint presentations as a visual aid.

To get your message across, you break it down into slides. Think of each slide as a canvas for the pictures, words, and shapes that will help you build your presentation.

You can also print out your presentation slides to give to your audience.

To launch PowerPoint go to the start screen and tap PowerPoint 2013

Getting Started

On your start screen click the powerpoint icon to start the application

Once PowerPoint has loaded, select a template below to start a new presentation or select blank to start your own. I'm going to go with mesh template below. Your most recently saved presentations are shown on the left hand orange pane below.

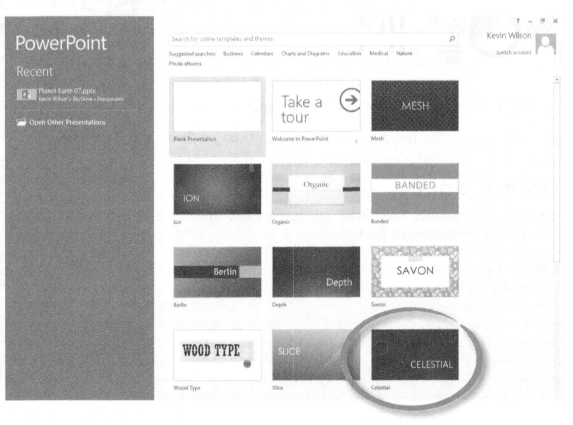

For this example, I am going to use the celestial template.

Lets take a look at PowerPoint's main screen. The tools are grouped into tabs called ribbons according to their function.

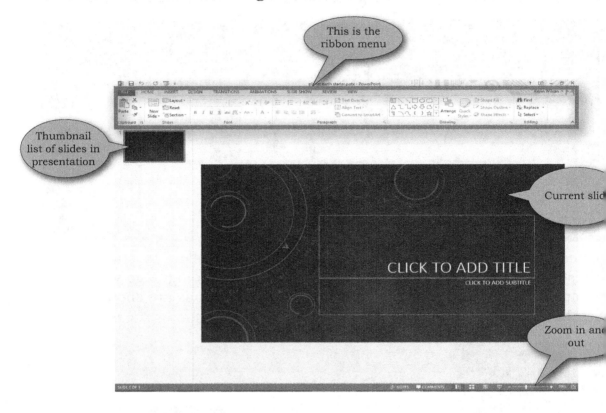

The Ribbon Menus

In PowerPoint, the tools are arranged in tabs according to their use.

Home Ribbon

All tools to do with text formatting, eg making text bold, changing fonts, and the most common tools

Insert Ribbon

All tools to do with inserting photos, graphics, tables, charts, sounds, movies, etc

Design Ribbon

All tools to do with the look of your slide, eg, the slide background.

Transitions Ribbon

All tools to add effects to show as slides change from one to the next

Animations Ribbon

All tools to add slide transitions and adding effects to text boxes.

Slideshow Ribbon

All tools to do with setting up your slideshow and running your presentation

Designing a Slide

In PowerPoint you can add photos or clipart, charts, diagrams, text, video, sound and animations.

Lets begin by designing our slide

In your slide click where it says 'click to add title'. This is a place holder for you to enter your title.

Add an Image

The easiest way to add an image to your slide is to first find the image in your pictures library from explorer on your desktop. The icon is on your task bar.

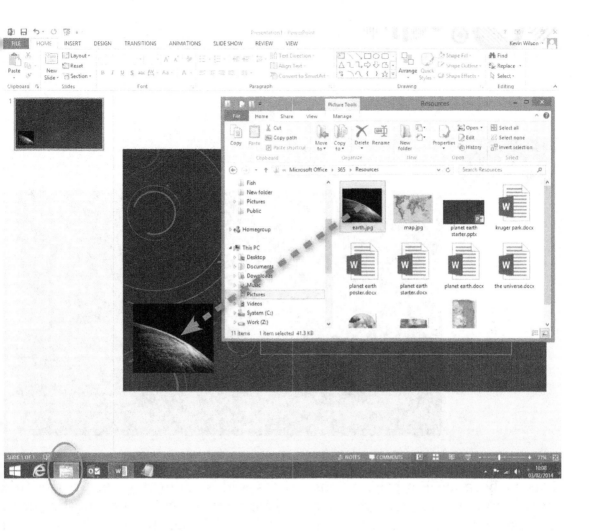

Resize an Images

If you click on your image you will notice a border surrounding your image.

In each corner and along the sides you will notice little squares.

These are resize handles. You can click and drag these to resize your image.

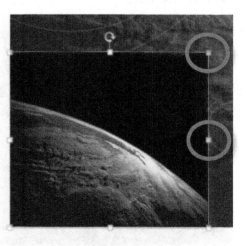

To resize the image, click and drag the resize handles until the image is the size you want.

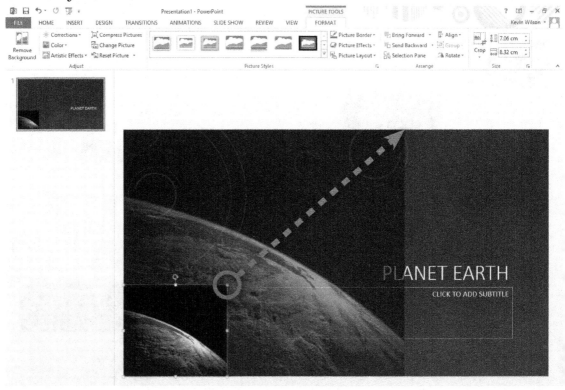

You will notice that when you have resized the image it covers the title. This is because PowerPoint constructs slides using layers. So the title "Planet Earth" will be on one layer and the image will be on another layer and because the image was inserted after the title, the image layer is on top of the title.

We can adjust this by changing the arrangement.

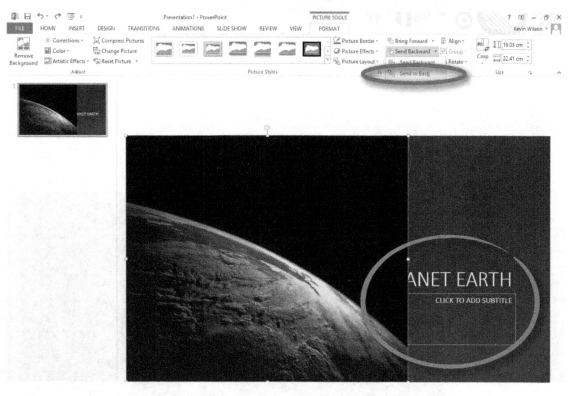

Click on the image and select the format ribbon. From the format ribbon click where it says 'send backward' because we want to put the image behind the title. From the drop down menu select 'send to back'

You will see the image drop behind the text layer.

This is useful if you have a lot of images and text that you need to lay out on your slide.

Add a New Slide

To continue building our presentation we need additional slides to show our information.

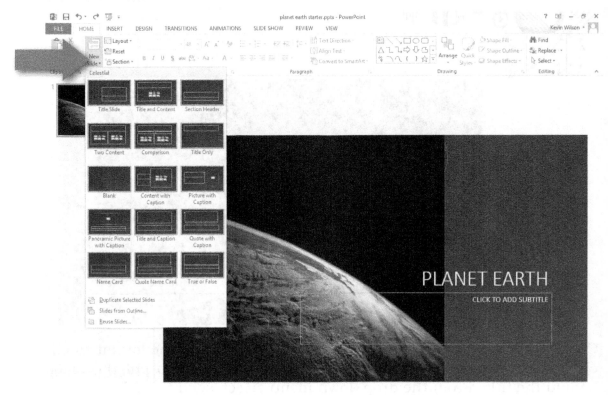

To add a new slide go to your home ribbon and click on icon 'New Slide'. Make sure you click on the text to reveal the drop down menu.

From the drop down menu select 'title and content' because we want a title on the slide but also we want to add some information in bullet points.

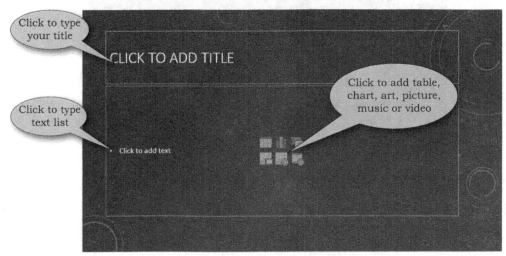

To add your text and titles just click in the text boxes and start typing your information as shown below.

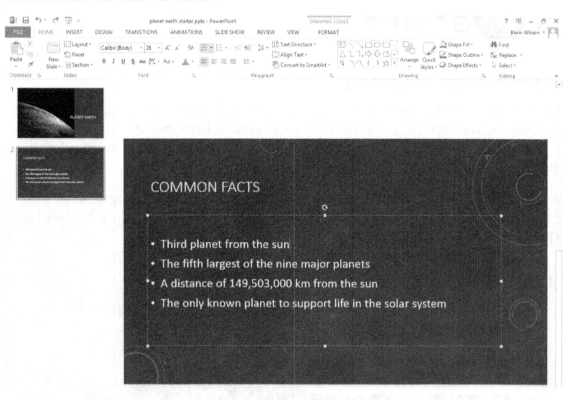

You can make text bigger by selecting it by clicking and dragging your mouse over the text so it is highlighted then click the home ribbon. From your home ribbon select the increase font size icon.

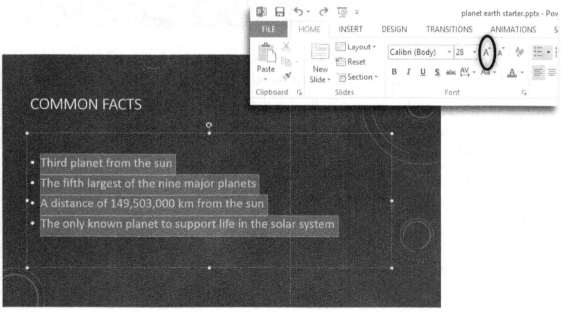

Adding Special Effects

You can adjust brightness and contrast, remove backgrounds, add animations and transitions between slides.

Adjusting Images

Sometimes it helps to make some minor adjustments to your photographs or images to make them blend into your slide a little better. You can change the brightness, contrast and colours of the images. You can do all this by experimenting with the adjustments on the format ribbon.

For example. If we go back to our first slide with the photograph of planet earth. We can make a few adjustments to this image to make it blend into the slide a little better.

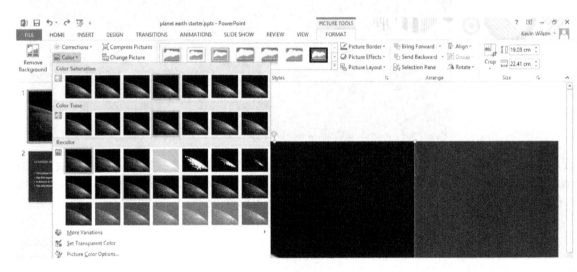

Click on the image on the slide and then click the format ribbon. On the format ribbon go to the adjustment section on the left hand side.

From the drop down menu, you can select 'color' if you want to change the colour blending of the image, eg select a blue/purple tint to match the background theme of the slide.

You can also do the same for other corrections such as brightness and contrast. Do this by selecting 'corrections' from the format ribbon instead of 'color'.

Another tip is to use the 'remove background' feature. This will only really work if the background of your image is the same colour or a plain background. It just helps to blend the photos into the slide a little better.

If you notice on the image of planet earth there is a black background. The 'remove background' feature will remove this.

To remove the background, make sure your image is selected and click 'remove background' from the format ribbon.

This will highlight all the bits PowerPoint is going to remove from the image in dark purple. You will also notice a box surrounding the area. Resize this box by clicking and dragging the resize handles until the box surrounds the area of the image you want to keep as shown above. Once you have done this click 'keep changes'

Slide Transitions

A slide transition is an animation or effect that is displayed when you move from one slide to the next.

To add transitions to PowerPoint slides click the slide you want to add the transition to then go to the transitions tab

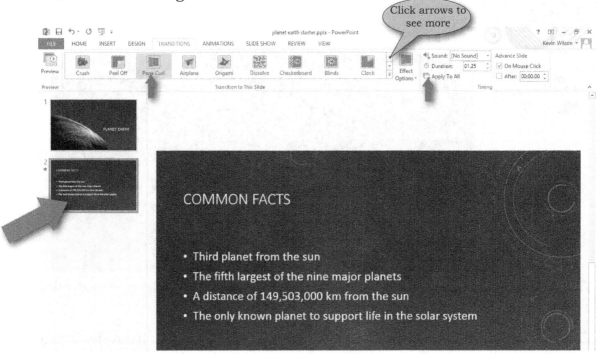

From the transitions tab you can select from a number of pre set transitions. If you click on a transition eg 'page curl', this will apply the transition to the selected slide.

To apply the transition to the whole presentation click 'apply to all' once you have selected your transition.

Slide Animations

Looking at the slide below, say you wanted each bullet point to appear one at a time instead of all at once.

You can do this by adding an animation to the text box. Click into the text box and select your animations ribbon.

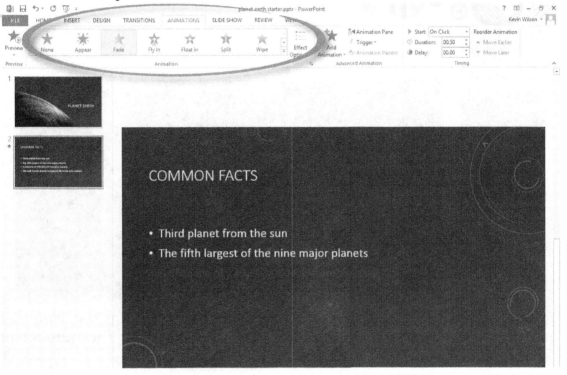

For this example, I am going to add a fade effect by selecting 'fade' from the animation pre sets circled above.

To view your presentation hit F5 on your keyboard.

Press Esc to return to PowerPoint

Insert a Table

We are going to add a table to a new slide. In this example I have added a new slide with 'title and content'

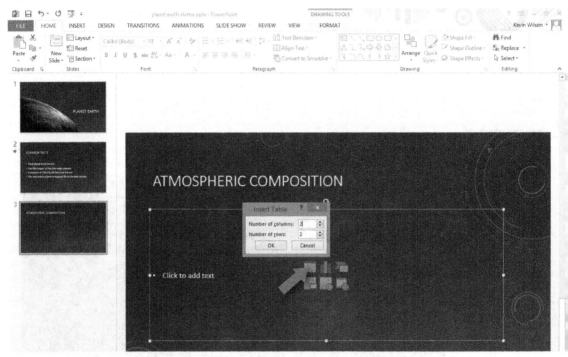

To add a table to this slide just click the table icon from the template as indicated above. In the dialog box that appears enter the number of columns and rows. This table is going to have 2 columns.

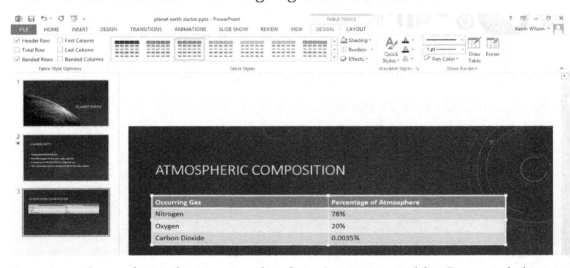

Occurring Gas	Percentage of Atmosphere
Nitrogen	78%
Oxygen	20%
Carbon Dioxide	0.0035%

Once you have done that, enter the data into your table. Press tab key to move between cells of the table. Don't worry about the number of rows, a new row will be inserted at the end of each row when entering your data.

You can also format your table using PowerPoint's pre designed templates. Click on the table and select the design ribbon.

Along the centre of the design ribbon you will see a number of pre sets, you can experiment with the designs by clicking on these. PowerPoint will automatically format the table using the colours and shadings in the templates.

Add a Chart

We are going to add a table to a new slide. In this example I have added a new slide with 'title and content'

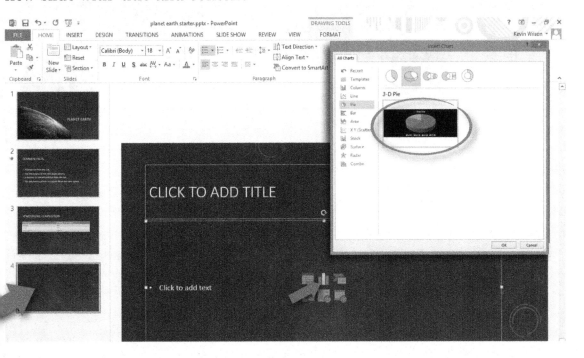

On the slide template click the chart icon circled above. From the dialog box that appears select the type of chart you want. In this example I am going to use a nice 3D pie chart. Click OK when you are done.

Enter the data in table form shown above.

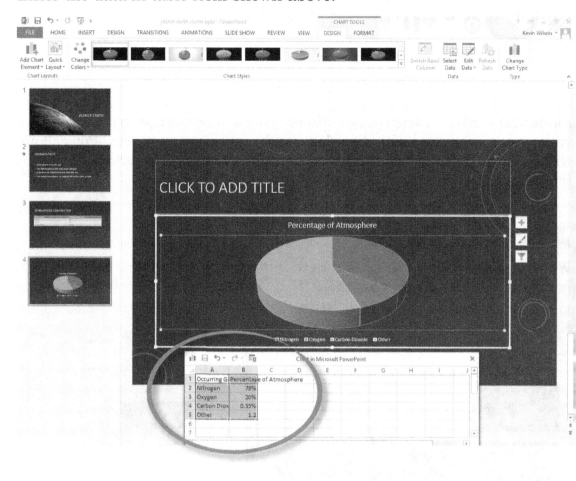

Print your Work

To print your document, click the File tab on the top left hand corner of the screen

In the screen below select the correct printer and number of copies you want.

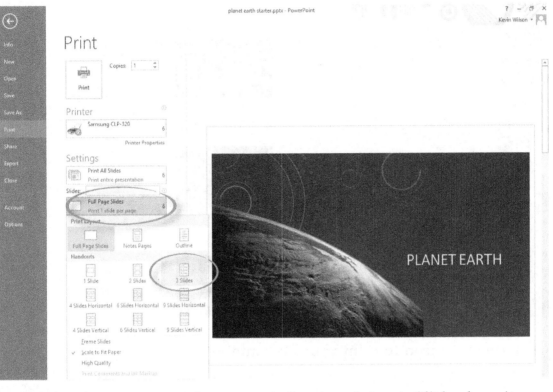

Then select how you want the presentation to print out. Click where it says "Full Page Slides".

This allows you to arrange more than one slide per page and with space to write notes. This is useful if you are giving a copy of your slides to your audience so they can follow your presentation as you speak and take notes.

A good one is 3 slides per page with writing space next to each, shown right.

Sometimes it is useful to select 'black and white' or greyscale printing if you do not have a colour printer.

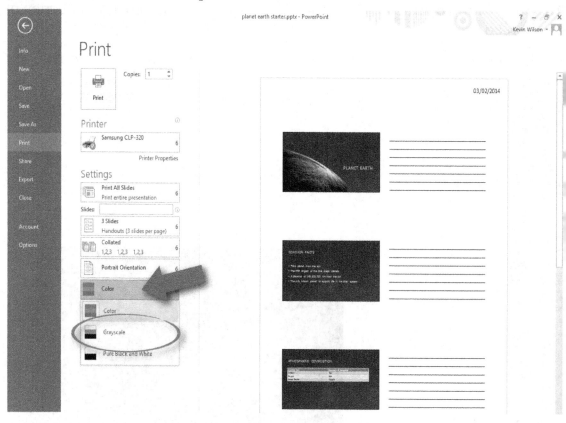

Click the print icon to print your presentation.

Chapter 6

Microsoft Excel 2013

Microsoft Excel is a spreadsheet program that allows you to store, organize, analyse and manipulate numerical data. It allows you to store and present it in tabular form or as a chart. To begin lets explore what a spreadsheet is.

What is a Spreadsheet?

A spreadsheet is made up of cells each identified by a reference.

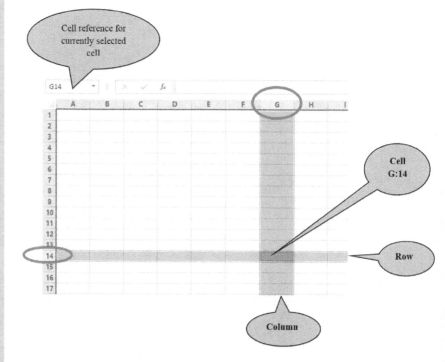

You can also select multiple cells at the same time. A group of cells is called as a cell range.

You can refer to a cell range using the cell reference of the first cell and the last cell in the range, separated by a colon.

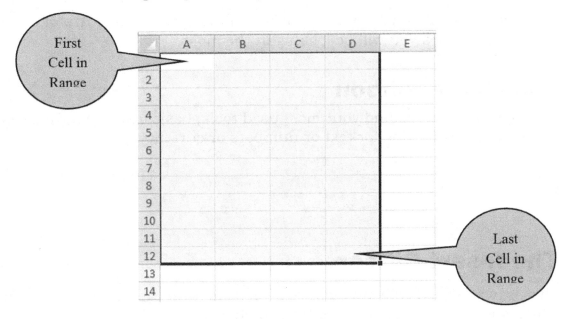

First Cell in Range

Last Cell in Range

This cell range would be A1:D12

Cell references are used when you start applying formulas to the numbers in your cells. In the example below to add two numbers you can enter a formula into cell C1.

Instead of typing in **=5+5** you would enter **=A1+B1**.

The theory is, if you enter the cell reference instead of the actual number you can perform calculations automatically and excel will recalculate all the numbers for you should you change anything.

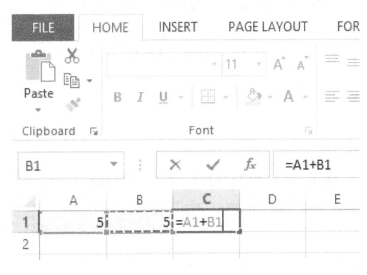

Eg if I wanted to change it to **5+6**, I would just change the number in cell B1 without rewriting the formula in C1. Now you can type any number in either cell A1 or B1 and it will add them up automatically.

The Ribbon

All the tools used in Microsoft excel are organised into ribbons loosely based on their function.

The most used ribbons are, home and formulas. For normal use of excel these are the ones you will be looking in the most.

The Home Ribbon

This is where you will find your most used tools, basic text formatting, cell borders, cell formatting for text or numbers or currency, etc.

The Insert Ribbon

This is where you will find all your objects you can insert into your spreadsheet such as shapes, tables and charts.

The Page Layout Ribbon

This is where you will find your page formatting functions, such as size of paper, colours & themes, paper orientation when printed, paper margins, etc

The Formulas Ribbon

This is where you will find your formulas, functions and your data manipulation tools. Sum functions, average, counting tools, etc

The View Ribbon

This is where you will find your view layouts, where you can zoom into your spreadsheet etc.

Creating Spreadsheets

To begin creating your spreadsheet start typing your data into the different cells on the spreadsheet.

Entering Data

In this example we are doing a basic scoring sheet.

	A	B	C	D
1		22-Apr	29-Apr	Total
2	Barbara	21	19	
3	Ann	10	21	
4	Flo	7	7	
5	Rose	9	12	
6	Emily		0	
7	Josie	21	21	
8	Lin			
9	Joan	19		
10	Eva	21	14	
11				

Simple Formatting

Sometimes it improves the readability of your spreadsheet to format the data in the cells.

For example, make the heading rows bold.

You can do this by selecting the heading row as shown right and click the bold icon.

Now because the headings are quite long and take up a lot of space, you can change the orientation of the headings to read vertically instead of horizontally. This helps save space and looks better when printed on a page.

You can do this by selecting the cells you want to change the orientation of. Then right click your mouse on the selection.

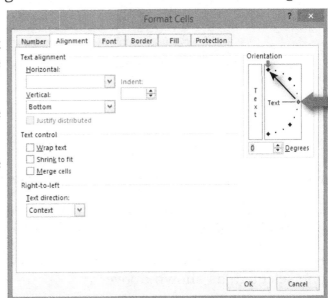

From the menu that appears, select 'format cells'. In the dialog box, click the alignment tab. From there go to the orientation section on the right of the dialog box.

Click the horizontal point and drag it up to the top (the vertical point).

Or you can enter 90 in the degrees box below.

You will see the headings are now oriented vertically

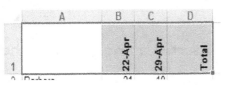

Resizing Rows and Columns

Resize a column or row by clicking and dragging the column or row divider lines

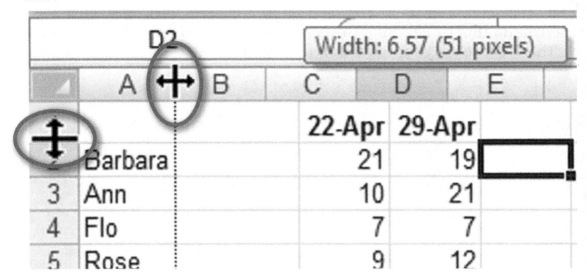

You can also double click on these lines to automatically size the row or column to the data that is in the cell.

Inserting Rows & Columns

To insert a row between Flo and Rose, right click with your mouse on the row Rose is in. In this case row 5

From the menu click insert. This will insert a blank row above Rose.

To insert a column it is exactly the same procedure except you select a column instead of a row.

Remember the new row or column is always inserted above or before the one selected, as shown above.

Using Formulas

Using formulas allow you to perform some calculations on the data you have entered. You can add up lists of data, multiply, subtract, find averages, plot charts all depending on what your spreadsheet is analysing.

If I wanted to add up all the scores in my score sheet, I could add another column called total and add a formula to add up the scores for the two weeks the player's played.

To do this I need to find the cell references for Barbara's scores.

Her scores are in row 2 and columns B and C circled below.

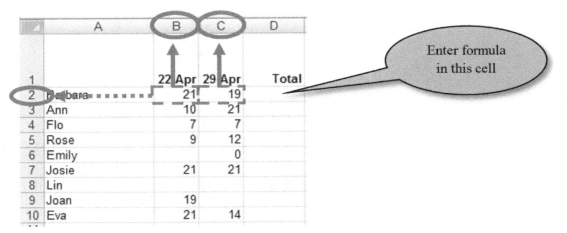

So the Cell references are B2 for her score of 21 and C2 for her score of 19.

So we enter into the cell under the heading 'total'

    = B2+C2

Remember all formulas must start with an equals sign (=).

Now a little tip. To save you entering the formula for each row you can replicate it instead.

If you click on the cell D2 where you entered the formula above you will notice on the bottom right of the box is a small square handle.

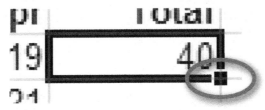

If you click and drag this down the rest of the column you want to use the formula.

D2	▼	⋮	✕	✓	*fx*	=C2+B2

◢	A	B 22-Apr	C 29-Apr	D Total
1				
2	Barbara	21	19	40
3	Ann	10	21	
4	Flo	7	7	
5	Rose	9	12	
6	Emily		0	
7	Josie	21	21	
8	Lin			
9	Joan	19		
10	Eva	21	14	
11				

Excel will automatically copy the formula and calculate the rest of the totals for you.

Using Functions

A function is a pre-defined formula. Excel provides over 300 different functions all designed to make analysing your data easier. We will start with some basic every day functions.

Say I wanted to add up the number of games played automatically. I could do this with a function.

Insert a new column after "29 Apr" into the spreadsheet and call it "Played". To do this right click on the D column (the 'Total' column) and from the menu click insert.

Make sure you have selected the cell you want the formula to appear in.

From the formulas ribbon click 'insert function'

	▼	⋮	✕	✓	*fx*	=

A	B 22-Apr	C 29-Apr	D Played	E Total
	21	9 =		40
	10	21		31

In the insert function dialog box select the count function from the list, click OK

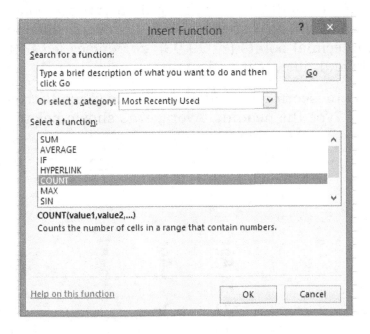

Now we need to tell the count function what we want it to count. We want to count the number of games played. Barbara's scores are in cells B1 and C1, so highlight these two by dragging your mouse over as circled below

	A	B	C	D	E
1		22 Apr	29 Apr	Played	Total
2	Barbara	21	19	2:C2)	40
3	Ann	10	21		31
4	Flo	7	7		14
5	Rose	9	12		21
6	Emily		0		0
7	Josie	21	21		42
8	Lin				0
9	Joan	19			19
10	Eva	21	14		35
11					
12					
13					
14					
15					
16					

Function Arguments

COUNT

Value1 B2:C2 = (21,19)
Value2 = number

= 2

Counts the number of cells in a range that contain numbers.

Value1: value1,value2,... are 1 to 255 arguments that can contain or refer to a variety of different types of data, but only numbers are counted.

Formula result = 2

Help on this function

Click OK. You can see she has played 2 games. Now we can replicate the formula as we did before.

Click and drag the small square on the bottom right hand side of the cell.

Drag it down over the rest of the column.

Apr	29-Apr	Played	Total
21	19	2	40
10	21		31
7	7		14
9	12		21
	0		0
21	21		42
			0
19			19
21	14		35

Types of Data

There are a number of different types of data you will come across using Excel. These can be numeric such as whole numbers called integers (eg 10), numbers with decimal points (eg 29.93), currencies (eg £4.67 or $43.76), as well as date and time, text and so on.

Going back to our scoring spreadsheet, we need another column for the average scores. Type the heading 'Average' as shown below.

| D2 | ▼ | ⋮ | ✕ ✓ *fx* | =E2/D2 |

◢	A	B 22-Apr	C 29-Apr	D Played	E Total	F Average
1						
2	Barbara	21	19	2	40	=E2/D2
3	Ann	10	21	2	31	
4	Flo	7	7	2	14	
5	Rose	9	12	2	21	
6	Emily		0	1	0	
7	Josie	21	21	2	42	
8	Lin			0	0	
9	Joan	19		1	19	
10	Eva	21	14	2	35	

We are going to work out the average scores over the number of games they players have played. In the Cell F2 enter the formula

```
Average = Total Score / Total number of Games Played
```

The total score is in E2 and the total number of games played is in D2. So we enter into F2

```
=E2 / D2
```

Use the forward slash for divide: **/**

Replicate the formula down the column as we did previously in the exercise.

Now the number format isn't as accurate as we want it. We need to tell excel that the data in this column is a number accurate to two decimal places. Highlight the cells you want to apply the number format to circled below.

In the home ribbon go up to number format (it will currently say 'general' in box). Click the little arrow.

From the drop down menu click number. This will format all the selected cells as a number with 2 decimal places.

It would be the same for if we were recording the fees paid by the players

Insert another column and call it fee. Say the fees are 4.50. When we enter 4.5 into the column excel thinks it's just a number, so we need to tell excel that it is currency.

Select all the data in the fee cell.

Go back to the home ribbon and click number format.

This time select currency from the drop down menu.

This will format all the numbers as a currency.

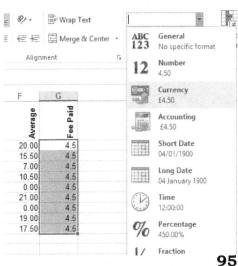

Formatting your Spreadsheet

To emphasise certain parts of your spreadsheet such as totals or headings you can apply borders and shading to cells or groups of cells.

Cell Alignment

This helps to align your data inside your cells and make it easier to read.

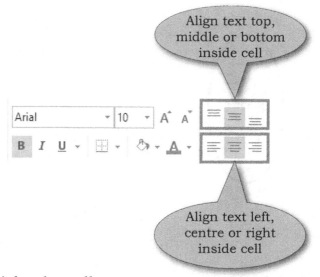

To do this highlight the cells you want to apply the alignment to, then select 'centre' from the alignment icons highlighted above. The top three align vertically in the cell, the bottom three align horizontally in the cell.

Text Format

As well as aligning the text inside your cell, you can apply bold or italic effects to make certain parts such as headings stand out.

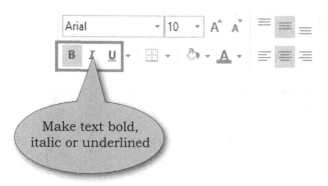

You can also change the font and size.

To do this in our spreadsheet highlight the headings ('22-Apr' to 'Fee Paid') and then click the bold icon highlighted below.

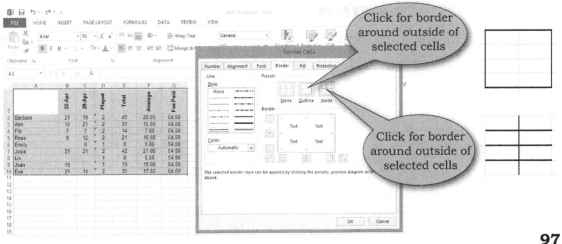

To align your text in the cells in the centre, again select the cells you want then click the centre icon as highlighted above.

Cell Borders

To apply borders to your spreadsheet. Select with your mouse the cells you want to format. In this case I am going to do the whole table. Right click on the selected cells and select 'format cells' from the menu.

I want the borders around all the cells both inside and the outline. So from the dialog box click 'outline' & 'inside'.

Now you can tweak the borders around individual cells. For example, it would make our spreadsheet easier to read if we separated the names from the scores and from the totals.

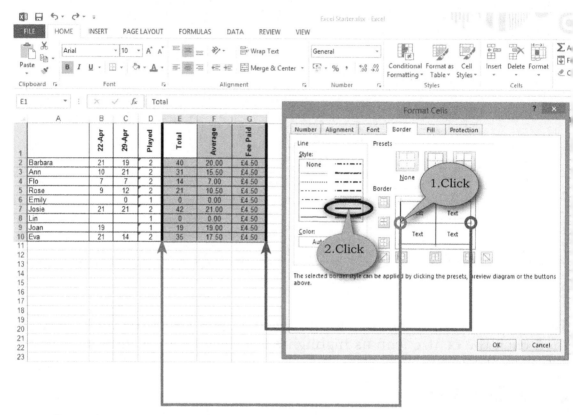

In the dialog box select the left most line under the border section. Then under the style section select the size of your line circled above.

Do this with the '22-Apr' column too.

First, highlight the column. Right click on selection and select 'format cells' from the menu...

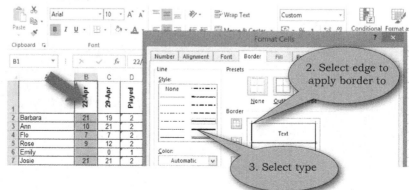

Adding a Chart

The easiest way to add a chart is to select from your spreadsheet a column you want for the X-Axis and a column you want for the Y-Axis.

I am going to do a chart on the total scores.

First select all the names in the first column. This will be the X-Axis on the chart.

	A	B	C	D	E	F	G
	10R x 1C					f_x	
1		22-Apr	29-Apr	Played	Total	Average	Fee
2	Barbara	21	19	2	40	20.00	£9.00
3	Ann	10	21	2	31	15.50	£9.00
4	Flo	7	7	2	14	7.00	£9.00
5	Rose	9	12	2	21	10.50	£9.00
6	Emily		0	1	0	0.00	£9.00
7	Josie	21	21	2	42	21.00	£9.00
8	Lin			0	0	#DIV/0!	£9.00
9	Joan	19		1	19	19.00	£9.00
10	Eva	21	14	2	35	17.50	£9.00
11							
12							
13							

Now hold down the control key on your keyboard. This allows you to multi-select.

While holding control, select the data in the total column with your mouse. This will be the Y-Axis on the chart.

Note the data in the names column is still highlighted

	A	B	C	D	E	F	G
	E1				Total		
1		22-Apr	29-Apr	Played	Total	Average	Fee
2	Barbara	21	19	2	40	20.00	£9.00
3	Ann	10	21	2	31	15.50	£9.00
4	Flo	7	7	2	14	7.00	£9.00
5	Rose	9	12	2	21	10.50	£9.00
6	Emily		0	1	0	0.00	£9.00
7	Josie	21	21	2	42	21.00	£9.00
8	Lin			0	0	#DIV/0!	£9.00
9	Joan	19		1	19	19.00	£9.00
10	Eva	21	14	2	35	17.50	£9.00
11							
12							
13							

Release the control key and go to the insert ribbon. In the centre of the ribbon you will find some different types of charts – line charts, column charts, pie charts.

I am going for a nice 3D column chart.

Click on it to add the chart.

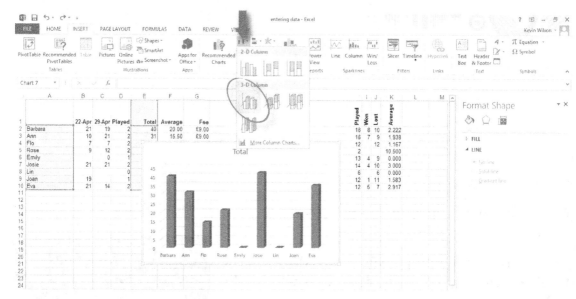

You are automatically taken to the design ribbon where you can select a style to auto-format the chart for you. Select a style that looks good. I'm going for a nice shaded effect.

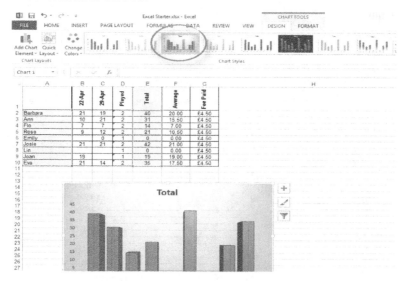

Printing your Spreadsheet

To print your document, click 'file' on the top left hand corner of the screen

In the menu down the left hand side select print.

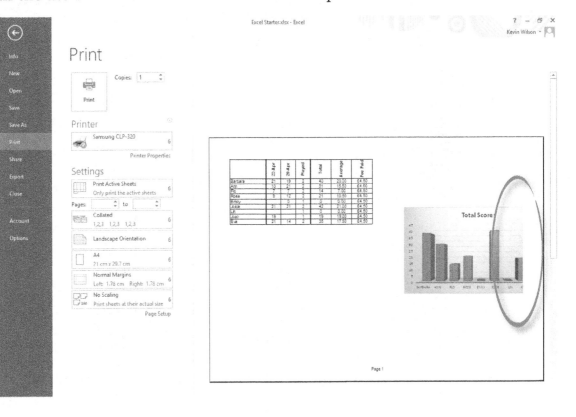

From here you can select the number of copies, the printer you're using, the range or pages you want to print. For example, if you just want to print the first page, last page etc. You can select landscape or portrait paper orientation - use landscape for printing spreadsheets. Paper size such as letter or A4, and margins, you can adjust from here. Scaling can be used to make the spreadsheet bigger or smaller to fit your page.

A tip when printing in excel is to keep an eye on the preview you can see on the right hand side of the screen above. Notice how the chart is cut off. Sometimes columns can be cut off too.

You can adjust this by going back to your spreadsheet. Do this by clicking the back arrow on the very top left of the screen.

This will take you back to your spreadsheet.

Excel will have placed dotted lines showing the edge of the page print area. Move the content you want on the page inside this area, either by moving charts by dragging or resizing columns etc.

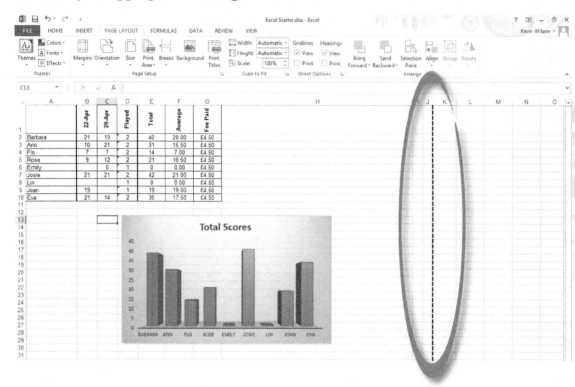

Also check your margins on the page layout ribbon, select narrow.

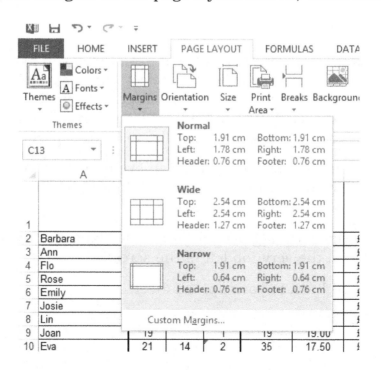

Now go to print your spreadsheet as before. (File -> Print)

Once you are happy with the print preview, print your document.

Click the print icon to send the spreadsheet to the printer.

Microsoft Outlook 2013

Microsoft Outlook 2013 is a personal information manager and email application available as a part of the Microsoft Office suite. It includes a calendar, contact list or address book as well as the ability to set reminders and make notes.

Outlook 2013 can be used as a stand-alone application for a personal email account, or can work with Microsoft Exchange for multiple users in an organization, such as shared mailboxes and calendars, public folders and meeting schedules.

Outlook 2013 organizes your emails, calendars and contacts all in one place. It all starts with your email account.

From there you can start working with emails, composing messages and replying to them. Storing the people you interact with in your contacts, so you never have to remember an email address or phone number and dealing with junk mail.

Let's start by taking a quick look at the basics.

Getting Started with Outlook

When you start Outlook you will see the main screen. In the following screen I've highlighted the main features in order to get started quickly and easily.

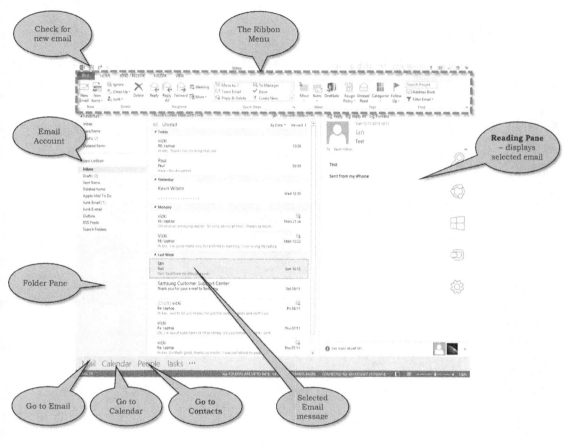

I find it a good idea to turn the reading pane off on your inbox. This helps with security so outlook doesn't automatically open unknown emails.

Select your inbox on the left hand side. Go to your view ribbon, click 'reading pane' and in the drop down box select 'off'.

This will remove the reading pane. To open any email, double click on the message and it will open in a separate window.

Main Ribbon Menus

All the main features and functions of Outlook are divided up into tabs called ribbons.

File Ribbon

This is where you can find all your printing, saving, import and account settings.

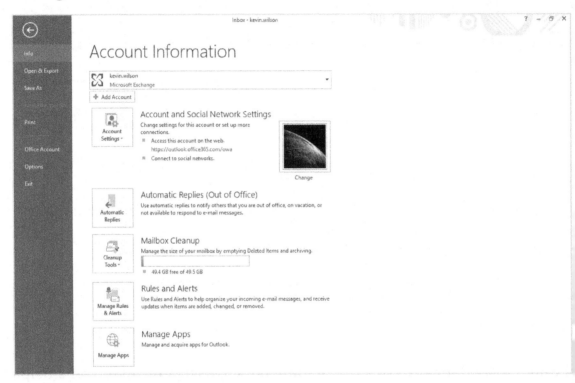

Home Ribbon

This is where you will find all your most used features such as composing new emails, reply and delete functions.

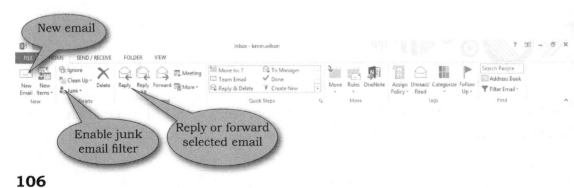

Send/Receive Ribbon

This is where you will find all your functions for manual sending and receiving email. Most of the time you won't need to use these except when you want to manually check for new emails, etc.

Folder Ribbon

The folder ribbon is where you will find functions to create folders for organizing your emails. For example, perhaps a folder for "Vicki" for all email from Vicki, or folder for "Accounts" for all email from accounting/banking, etc.

View Ribbon

The view ribbon allows you to sort your emails by name or date and allows you to turn on or off different sections, such as the reading pane.

Email Message Ribbons

When you go to reply to an email message or compose a new one you will find that the message window has its own set of ribbons.

Message Ribbon

Insert Ribbon

Use this ribbon if you want to insert shapes, charts, tables, calendar appointments, hyperlinks or any kind of symbol.

Options Ribbon

Use this ribbon to enable the BCC field, set up delivery reports, page colours and effects.

Format Text Ribbon

Use this ribbon to format your text. To change fonts, align text left or right, change font size, change line or paragraph indent, create bulleted and numbered lists, etc

Review Ribbon

The review ribbon has features to check spelling and grammar. It also has statistical features such as word counts. You can lookup certain words and find synonyms for words using a thesaurus. Translate into different languages etc.

Sending Email

From the home ribbon click New E-mail.

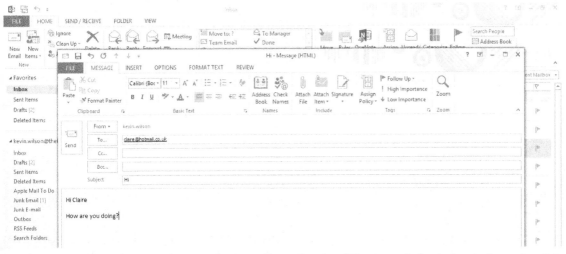

In the window that appears enter the email address of your recipient in the To field. You can do this by typing in the address and outlook will search your contacts and display suggested addresses.

You can also add email addressed by clicking the To field and selecting the recipients from your address book. Note you can select more than one if you want to send the same message to other people.

The Cc field is for carbon copies and is used to send a copy of the message to other people.

The Bcc field is for blind carbon copies - you can enable this on the options ribbon if it isn't there. This works like the CC field except the recipient can't see the addresses of the other people the message has been sent to.

Then type your message in at the bottom.

Attachments

You can also send attachments, such as photos or documents. To do this click on the Attach File icon that looks like a paper clip.

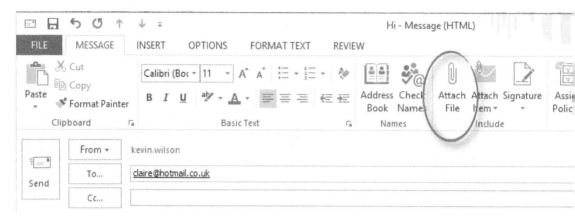

Select your file from the insert file dialog box and click insert. You can select more than one file by holding down the control (ctrl) key on your keyboard.

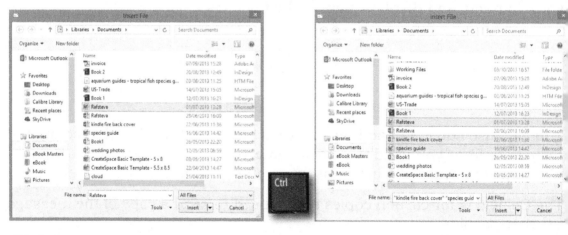

Click insert.

Once you are happy with your message, click Send.

Calendar

To start your Calendar, click the calendar icon located at the bottom left of your screen.

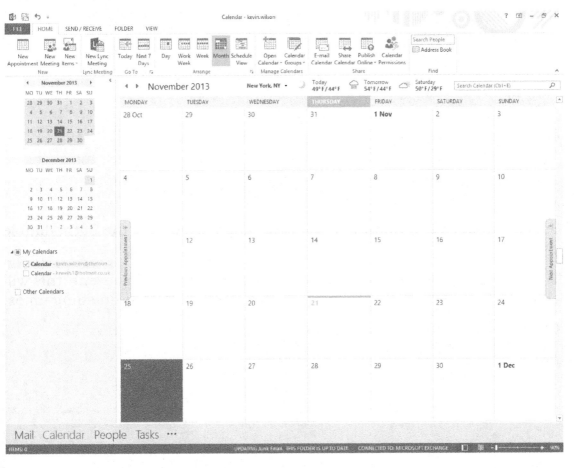

Once you are in your calendar you can see the calendar with months and dates. It is personal preference but I find it easier to work within month view.

You can do this by clicking on the month icon on your home ribbon shown as shown above.

Add Appointment

The quickest way to add an event or appointment is to double click the day.

So, for example, if you wanted to add an appointment on the 25th, double click 25.

The following dialog appears, Remove the tick from "all day event" this will allow you to enter specific times; start time and estimated finishing times.

Click 'Save & Close' when you have finished.

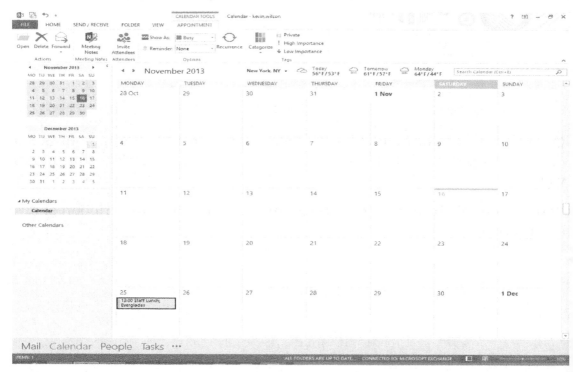

In the screen above you can see the appointment has been added.

Dealing with Junk Mail

If you have been using the internet you will no doubt have received junk mail in the past. Mail advertising products from unknown senders that you wonder how they got your email address.

Outlook has a junk mail filter. It is good practice to enable this filter as suspicious emails used for phishing personal details, etc.

To enable the filter click 'junk' from the home ribbon

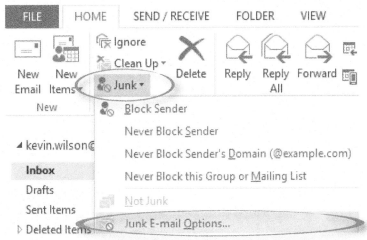

In the dialog box that pops up select 'low: move the most obvious junk email to the junk email folder'

Also select 'disable links...' and 'warn about suspicious domains...'.

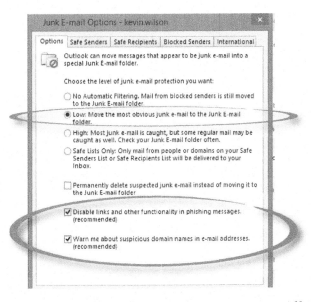

This helps to filter out emails sent from scammers etc. All these emails will be filtered into your junk mail box instead of your inbox.

Chapter 7: Microsoft Outlook 2013

CPSIA information can be obtained
at www.ICGtesting.com
Printed in the USA
LVOW03s1324301015

460447LV00010B/155/P